school - 학교   2
travel - 여행   5
transport - 운반   8
city - 도시   10
landscape - 풍경   14
restaurant - 레스토랑   17
supermarket - 수퍼마켓   20
drinks - 음료수   22
food - 음식   23
farm - 농장   27
house - 집   31
living room - 응접실   33
kitchen - 부엌   35
bathroom - 욕실   38
child's room - 아이들 방   42
clothing - 의복   44
office - 사무실   49
economy - 경제   51
occupations - 직업   53
tools - 연장   56
musical instruments - 악기   57
zoo - 동물원   59
sports - 스포츠   62
activities - 활동   63
family - 가족   67
body - 몸통   68
hospital - 병원   72
emergency - 응급상황   76
Earth - 지구   77
clock - 시계   79
week - 주간   80
year - 년도   81
shapes - 형태   83
colours - 색   84
opposites - 반대   85
numbers - 숫자   88
languages - 언어   90
who / what / how - 누가 / 무엇이 / 어떻게   91
where - 어디에   92

Impressum
Verlag: BABADADA GmbH, Nedderfeld 112 , 22529 Hamburg
Geschäftsführer / Verlagsleitung: Harald Hof
Druck: Books on Demand GmbH, In de Tarpen 42, 22848 Norderstedt

Imprint
Publisher: BABADADA GmbH, Nedderfeld 112 , 22529 Hamburg, Germany
Managing Director / Publishing direction: Harald Hof
Print: Books on Demand GmbH, In de Tarpen 42, 22848 Norderstedt

AF200074

school
학교

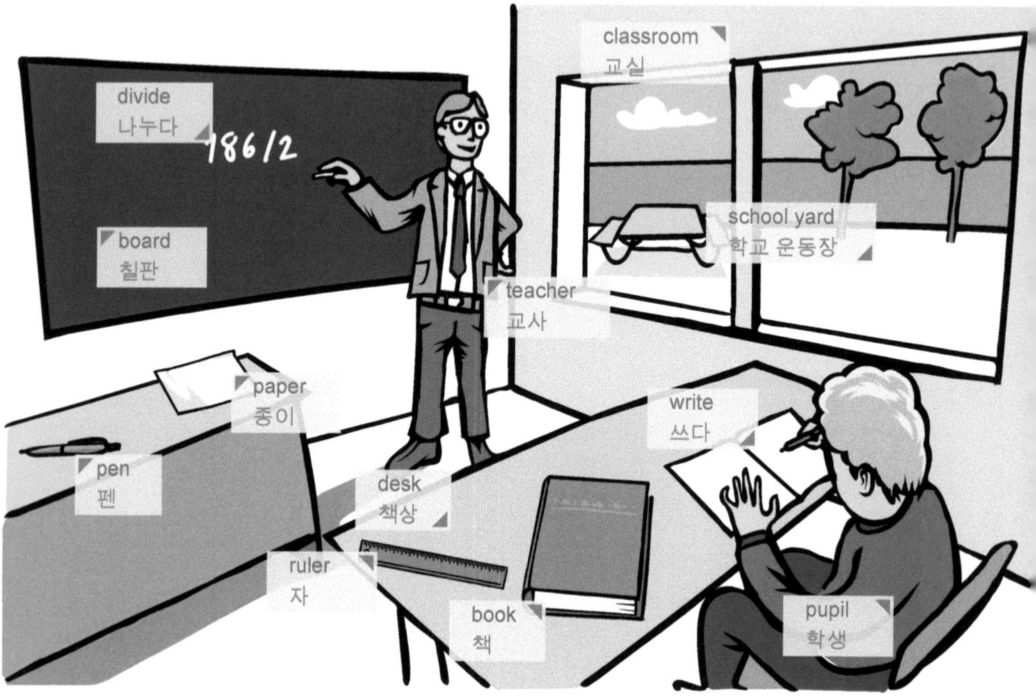
classroom
교실
divide
나누다
186/2
board
칠판
school yard
학교 운동장
teacher
교사
paper
종이
write
쓰다
pen
펜
desk
책상
ruler
자
book
책
pupil
학생

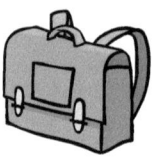

satchel
책가방

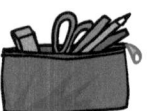

pencil case
필통

pencil
연필

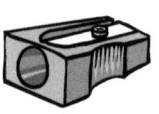

pencil sharpener
연필깎이

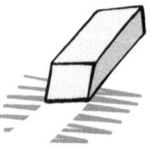

rubber
지우개

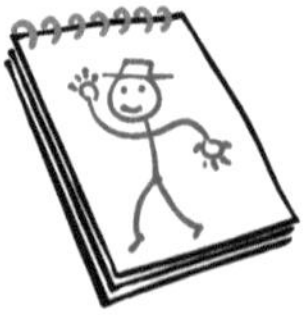

drawing pad
스케치북

drawing

그림

paintbrush

붓

paint box

그림물감 통

scissors

가위

glue

풀

exercise book

연습장

homework

숙제

number

숫자

add

더하다

subtract

빼다

multiply

곱하다

calculate

계산하다

letter

글자

alphabet

알파벳

word

낱말

text

텍스트

read

읽다

chalk

분필

lesson

수업시간

register

출석부

exam

시험

certificate

증명서

school uniform

교복

education

교육

encyclopedia

백과사전

university

대학교

microscope

현미경

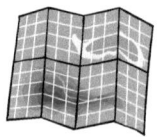

map

지도

waste-paper basket

휴지통

school - 학교

hotel
호텔

Grand

hostel
호스텔

ROOMS

bureau de change
환전소

EXCHANGE

car
자동차

language

언어

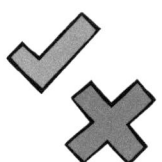

yes / no

예 / 아니오

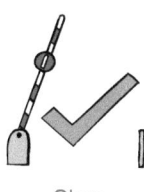

Okay

좋아

hello

안녕

translator

번역가

Thank you

고마워, 고마워요

how much is...?

... 얼마입니까?

I do not understand

나는 이해하지 못합니다

problem

문제

Good evening!

안녕하세요!

Good morning!

안녕하세요!

Good night!

잘자요!

bye bye

또 만나요

direction

방향

luggage

수하물

bag

가방

backpack

배낭

guest

손님

room

방

sleeping bag

침낭

tent

텐트

tourist information

여행 안내

beach

해변

credit card

신용카드

breakfast

아침식사

lunch

점심식사

dinner

저녁식사

ticket

승차권

lift

승강기

stamp

우표

border

경계

customs

세관

embassy

대사관

visa

비자

passport

여권

travel - 여행

transport
운반

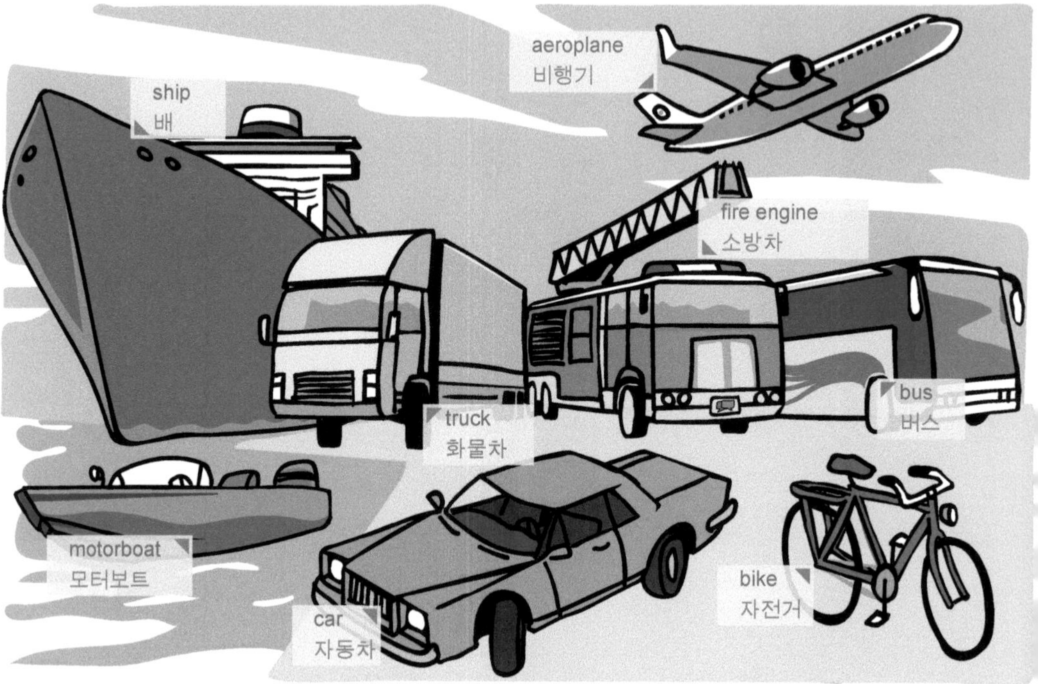
aeroplane
비행기
ship
배
fire engine
소방차
bus
버스
truck
화물차
motorboat
모터보트
bike
자전거
car
자동차

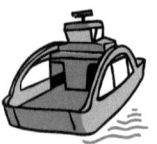

ferry
페리

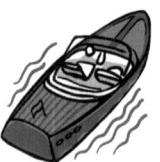

boat
보트

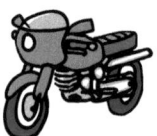

motorbike
오토바이

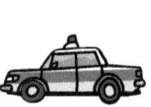

police car
경찰차

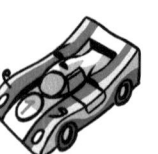

racing car
경주차

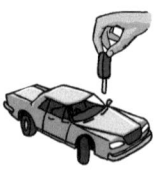

rental car
렌트카

car sharing

카셰어링

breakdown truck

견인차

refuse truck

쓰레기차

motor

모터

fuel

연료

petrol station

주유소

traffic sign

교통 표지

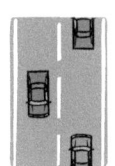

traffic

교통

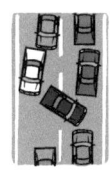

traffic jam

교통 정체

car park

주차장

train station

기차역

tracks

트랙터

train

기차

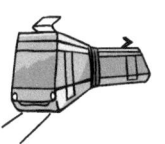

tram

전차

carriage

객차

helicopter

헬리콥터

airport

공항

tower

타워

passenger

승객

container

컨테이너

carton

상자

cart

카트

basket

바구니

take off / land

출발하다 / 도착하다

city

도시

village

마을

city centre

도심

house

집

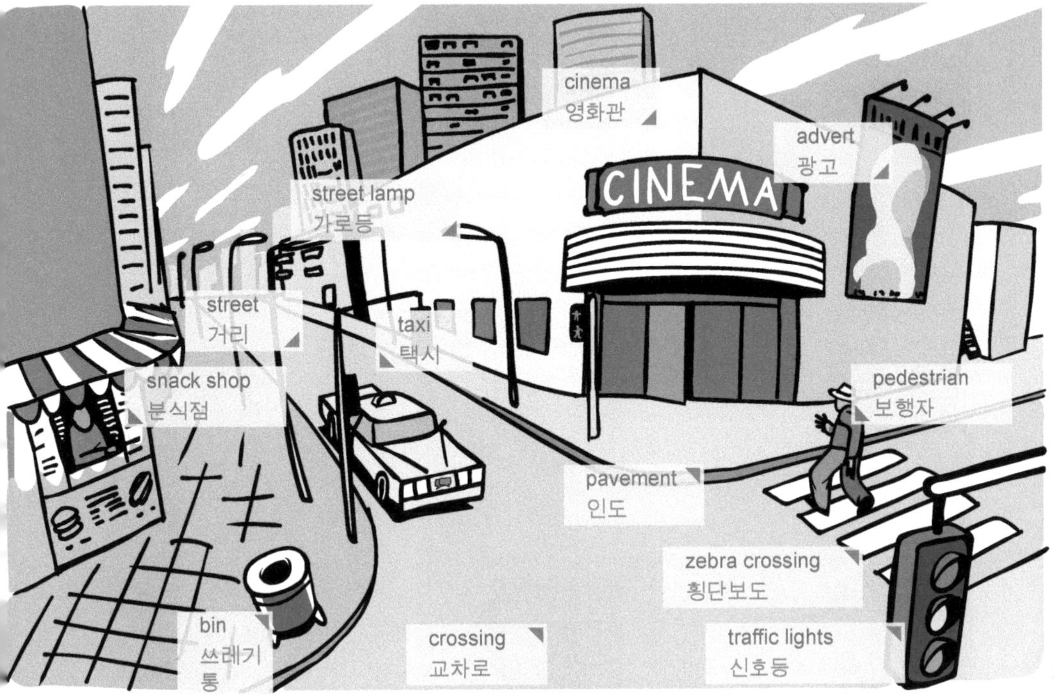
cinema
영화관
advert
광고
CINEMA
street lamp
가로등
street
거리
taxi
택시
snack shop
분식점
pedestrian
보행자
pavement
인도
zebra crossing
횡단보도
bin
쓰레기
통
crossing
교차로
traffic lights
신호등

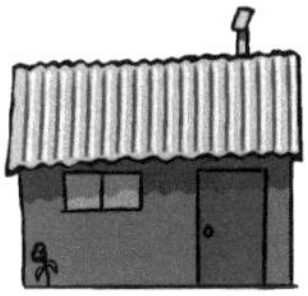

hut

오두막

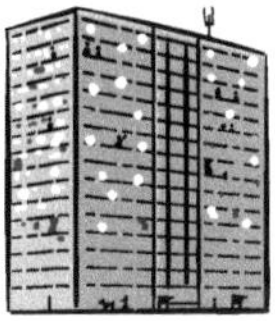

flat

주택

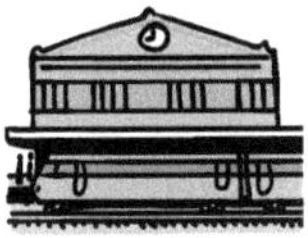

train station

기차역

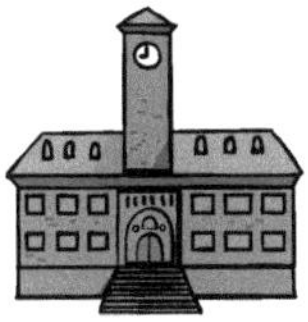

town hall

시청

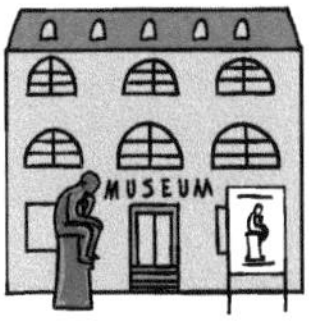
MUSEUM

museum

박물관

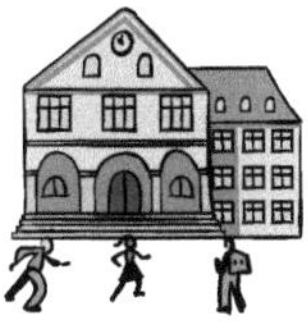

school

학교

university

대학교

bank

은행

hospital

병원

hotel

호텔

pharmacy

약국

office

사무실

book shop

서점

shop

상점

florist's

꽃가게

supermarket

수퍼마켓

market

시장

department store

백화점

fishmonger's

생선가게

shopping centre

쇼핑 센터

harbour

항구

park

공원

bench

벤치

bridge

다리

stairs

계단

underground

지하철

tunnel

터널

bus stop

버스 정류장

bar

바

restaurant

레스토랑

postbox

우체통

street sign

도로 표지판

parking meter

주차료 징수기

zoo

동물원

swimming pool

수영장

mosque

모스크 사원

farm

농장

pollution

환경오염

graveyard

공동묘지

church

교회

playground

놀이터

temple

절

landscape
풍경

signpost
이정표

way
길

meadow
초원

stone
돌

hiker
도보여행자

tree
나무

river
강

grass
잔디

flower
꽃

valley

계곡

hill

산

lake

호수

forest

숲

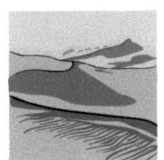

desert

사막

volcano

화산

castle

성

rainbow

무지개

mushroom

버섯

palm tree

야자나무

mosquito

모기

fly

파리

ant

개미

bee

벌

spider

거미

beetle

딱정벌레

frog

개구리

squirrel

다람쥐

hedgehog

고슴도치

hare

토끼

owl

부엉이

bird

새

swan

백조

boar

맷돼지

deer

사슴

moose

순록

dam

댐

wind turbine

풍력 터빈

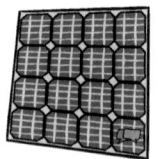

solar panel

태양광 전지판

climate

기후

waiter
웨이터

menu
메뉴

chair
의자

soup
수프

pizza
피자

cutlery
수저

tablecloth
테이블보

starter
전채요리

main course
주요리

dessert
후식

drinks
음료수

food
음식

bottle
병

fast food

인스턴트 식품

street food

길거리음식

teapot

찻주전자

sugar bowl

설탕통

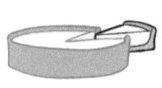

portion

인분

espresso machine

에스프레소 머신

high chair

높은 의자

bill

계산서

tray

쟁반

knife

칼

fork

포크

spoon

숟가락

teaspoon

찻숟가락

serviette

냅킨

glass

유리잔

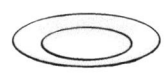

plate

접시

soup plate

수프 그릇

saucer

컵 받침

sauce

소스

salt pot

소금통

pepper mill

후추통

vinegar

식초

oil

기름

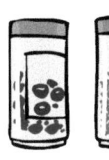

spices

양념

ketchup

케첩

mustard

겨자

mayonnaise

마요네즈

supermarket
수퍼마켓

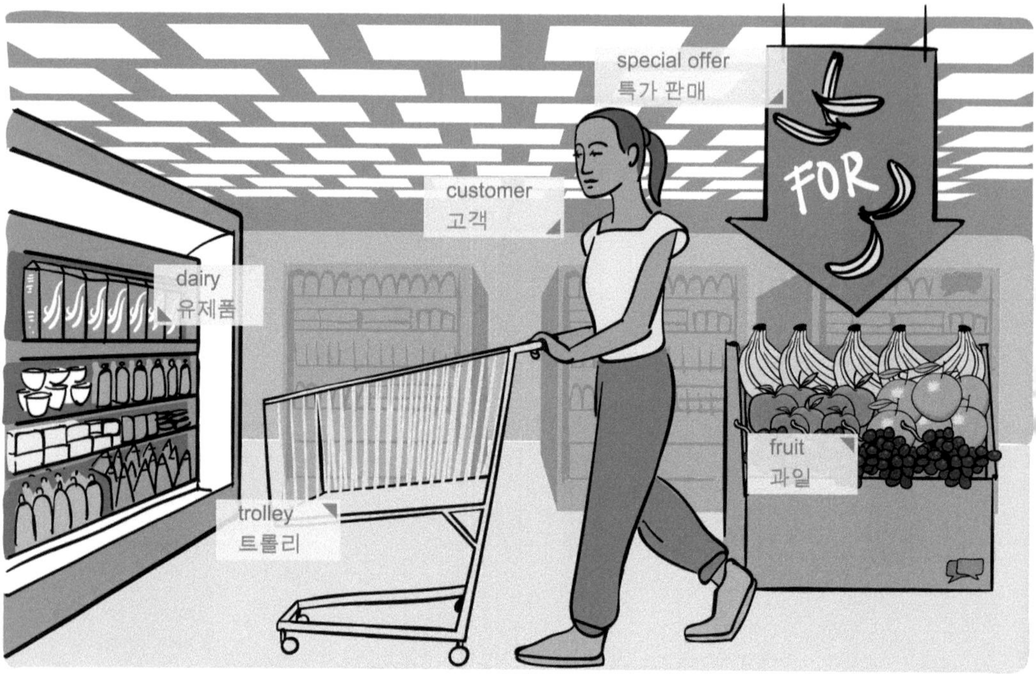

special offer
특가 판매
FOR
customer
고객
dairy
유제품
fruit
과일
trolley
트롤리

BUTCHERS

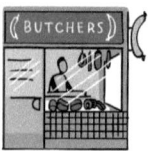

butcher´s

정육점

BAKERY

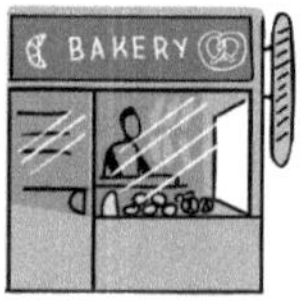

baker´s

빵집

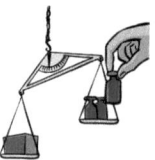

weigh

무게가 나가다

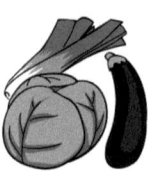

vegetables

채소

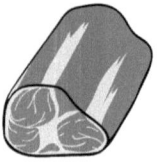

meat

고기

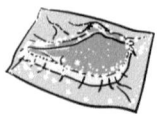

frozen food

냉동식품

cold meat
냉육

tinned food
통조림

washing powder
가루 세제

sweets
달콤한 간식

household products
가정용품

cleaning products
세척제

salesperson
판매원

till
계산대

cashier
계산원

shopping list
구매목록

opening hours
문 여는 시간

wallet
지갑

credit card
신용카드

bag
가방

plastic bag
비닐 봉투

water

물

juice

주스

milk

우유

coke

콜라

wine

와인

beer

맥주

alcohol

술

cocoa

카카오

tea

차고

coffee

커피

espresso

에스프레소

cappuccino

카푸치노

banana

바나나

apple

사과

orange

오렌지

melon

수박

lemon

레몬

carrot

당근

garlic

마늘

bamboo

대나무

onion

양파

mushroom

버섯

nuts

견과류

noodles

국수

spaghetti

스파게티

rice

쌀

salad

샐러드

chips

감자칩

fried potatoes

감자튀김

pizza

피자

hamburger

햄버거

sandwich

샌드위치

cutlet

커틀렛

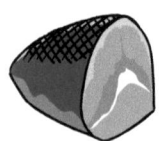

ham

햄

salami

살라미

sausage

소시지

chicken

닭

roast

구이

fish

생선

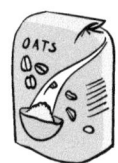

porridge oats

오트밀

muesli

뮤슬리

cornflakes

콘플레이크

flour

밀가루

croissant

크루아상

bread roll

롤빵

bread

빵

toast

토스트

biscuits

비스킷

butter

버터

curd

응유

cake

케이크

egg

달걀

fried egg

계란 후라이

cheese

치즈

food - 음식

ice cream

아이스크림

sugar

설탕

honey

꿀

jam

잼

chocolate spread

누가 크림

curry

카레

farm
농장

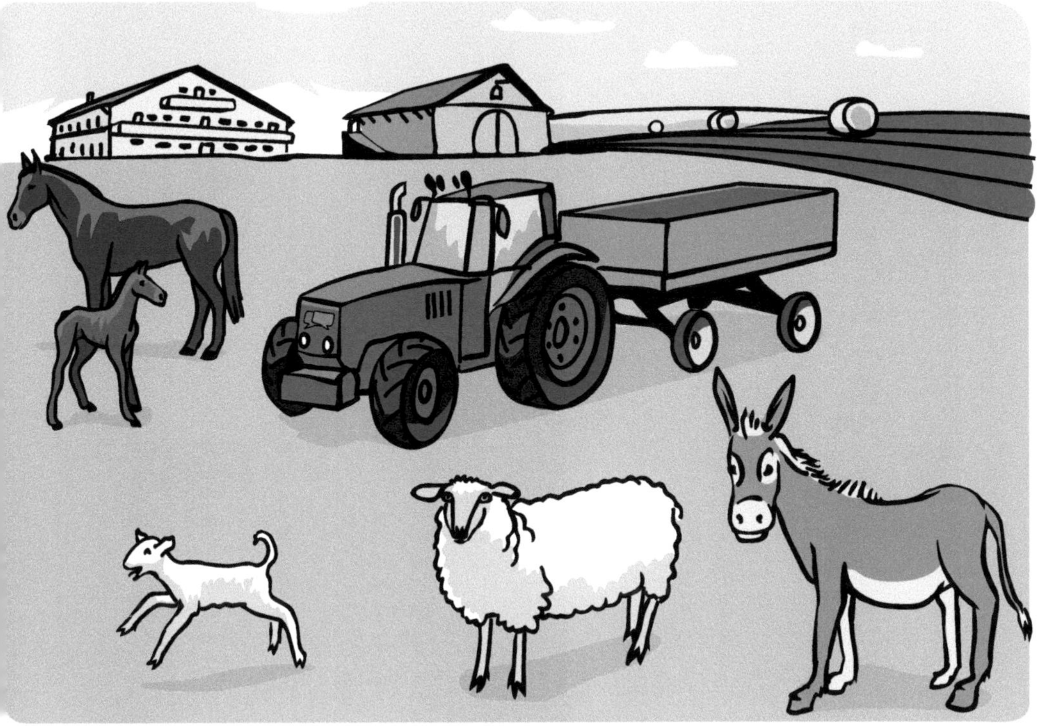

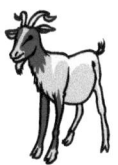

goat

염소

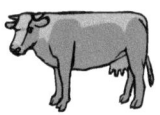

cow

암소

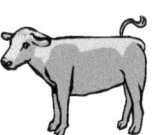

calf

송아지

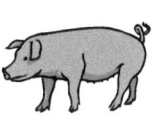

pig

돼지

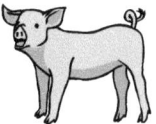

piglet

새끼 돼지

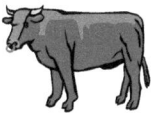

bull

황소

goose
거위

duck
오리

chick
병아리

hen
암탉

cock
수탉

rat
쥐

cat
고양이

mouse
생쥐

ox
황소

dog
개

doghouse
개집

garden hose
정원용 호스

watering can
물뿌리개

scythe
큰 낫

plough
쟁기

sickle
낫

hoe
괭이

pitchfork
쇠스랑

axe
도끼

wheelbarrow
외바퀴 손수레

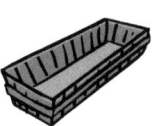

trough
여물통

milk can
우유 캔

sack
부대

fence
울타리

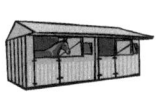

stable
축사

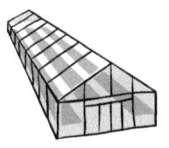

greenhouse
비닐하우스

soil
땅

seed
씨앗

fertilizer
거름

combine harvester
콤바인

harvest

수확하다

harvest

수확

yams

참마

wheat

밀

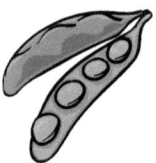

soy

콩

potato

감자

corn

옥수수

rapeseed

유채씨

fruit tree

과일나무

cassava

카사바

cereals

곡식

house
집

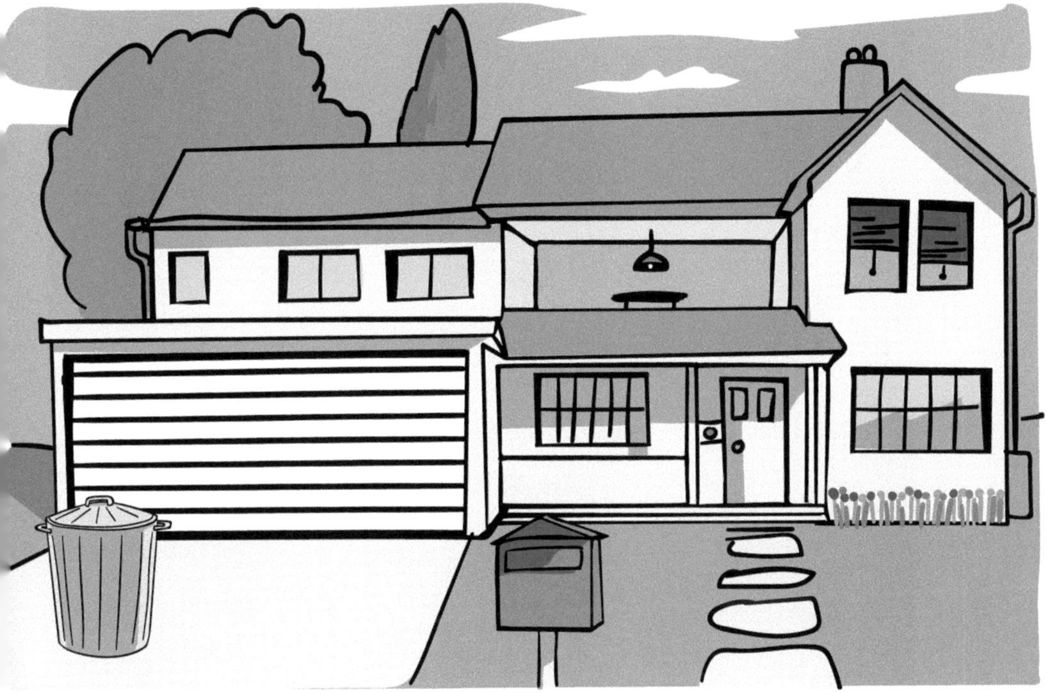

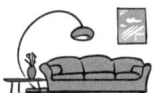

living room
응접실

bathroom
욕실

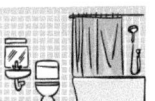

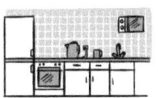

kitchen
부엌

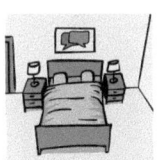

bedroom
침실

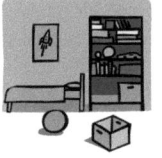

child's room
아이들 방

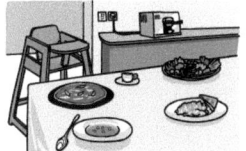

dining room
식사실

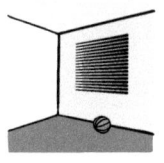

floor

바닥

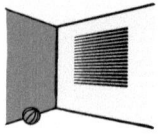

wall

벽

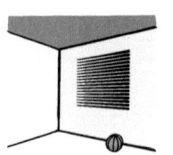

ceiling

천장

cellar

지하실

sauna

사우나

balcony

발코니

terrace

테라스

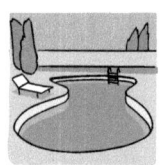

pool

수영장

lawn mower

잔디 깎는 기계

sheet

침대 시트

bedspread

이불

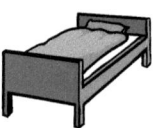

bed

침대

broom

빗자루

bucket

양동이

switch

스위치

living room
응접실

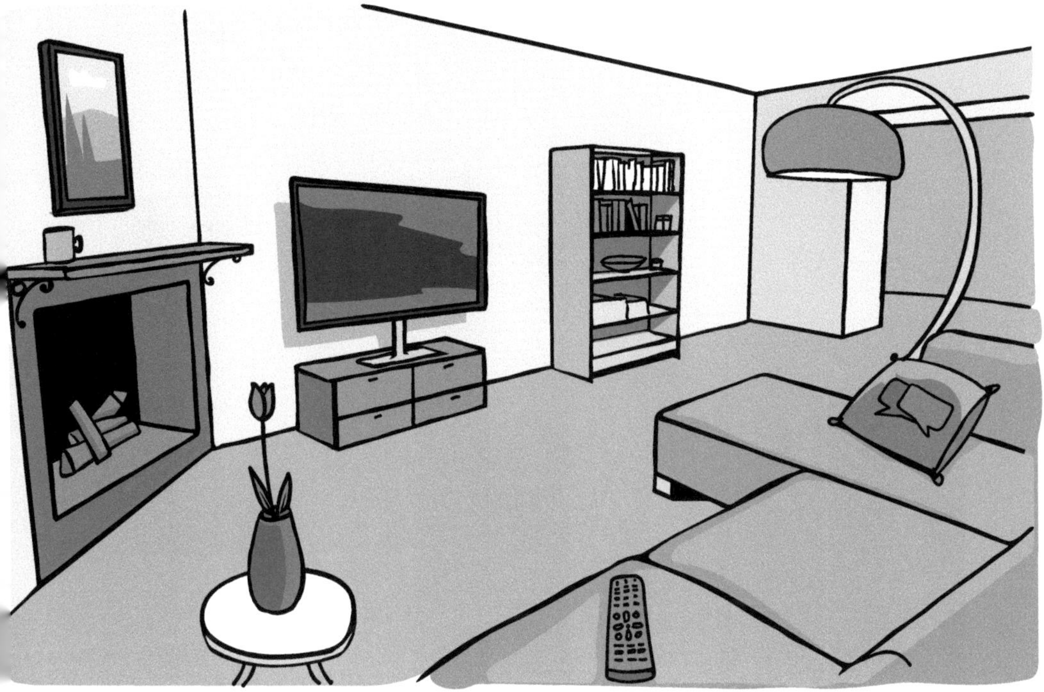

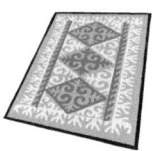

carpet

카페트

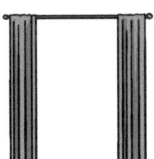

curtain

커튼

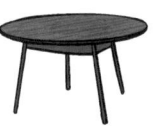

table

탁자

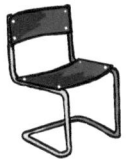

chair

의자

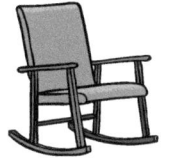

rocking chair

흔들의자

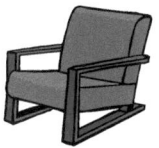

armchair

안락의자

book

책

blanket

담요

decoration

장식

firewood

땔감나무

film

영화

hi-fi equipment

하이파이 기기

key

열쇠

newspaper

신문

painting

회화

poster

포스터

radio

라디오

notepad

노트

hoover

진공청소기

cactus

선인장

candle

초

kitchen
부엌

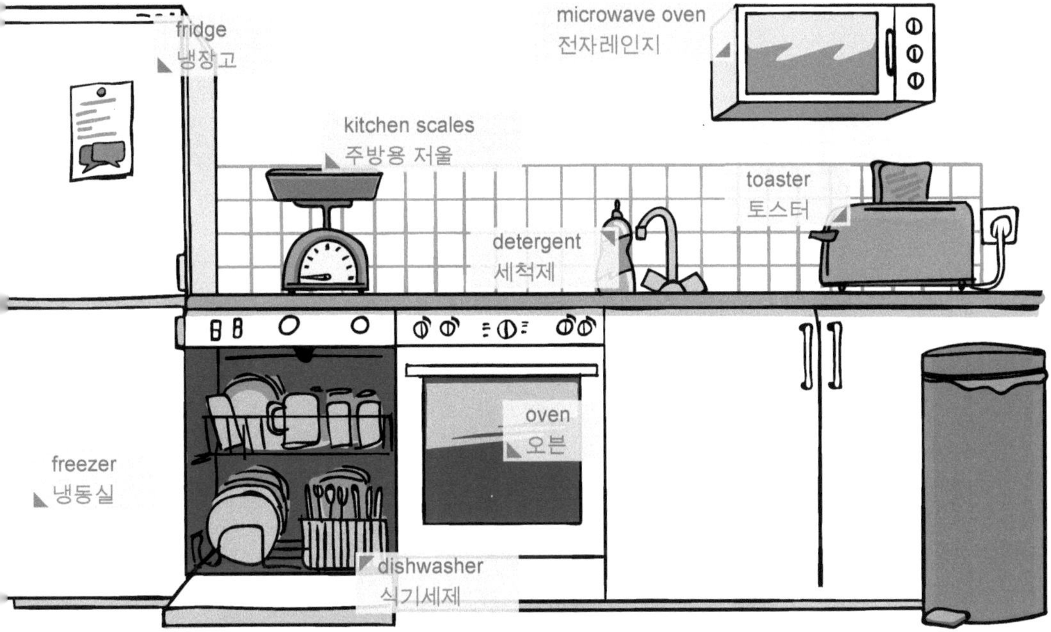
fridge
냉장고
microwave oven
전자레인지
kitchen scales
주방용 저울
toaster
토스터
detergent
세척제
oven
오븐
freezer
냉동실
dishwasher
식기세제

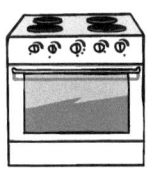

cooker

쿠커

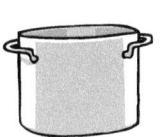

pot

냄비

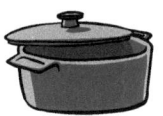

cast-iron pot

주철 냄비

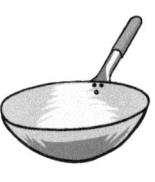

wok / kadai

웍 / 카다이 냄비

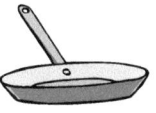

pan

프라이팬

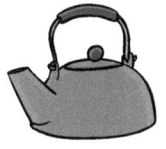

kettle

주전자

steamer

찜기

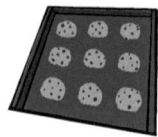

baking tray

오븐 구이용 쟁반

crockery

그릇

mug

머그

bowl

양푼이

chopsticks

젓가락

ladle

국자

spatula

주걱

whisk

거품기

strainer

여과기

sieve

체

grater

강판

mortar

절구

barbecue

바베큐

open fire

화덕

chopping board

도마

rolling pin

밀방망이

corkscrew

코르크 병따개

can

캔

can opener

캔 따개

pot holder

냄비 받침

sink

개수대

brush

솔

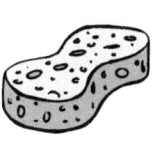

sponge

수세미

blender

블렌더

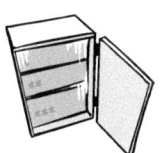

deep freezer

냉동고

baby bottle

젖병

tap

수도꼭지

bathroom
욕실

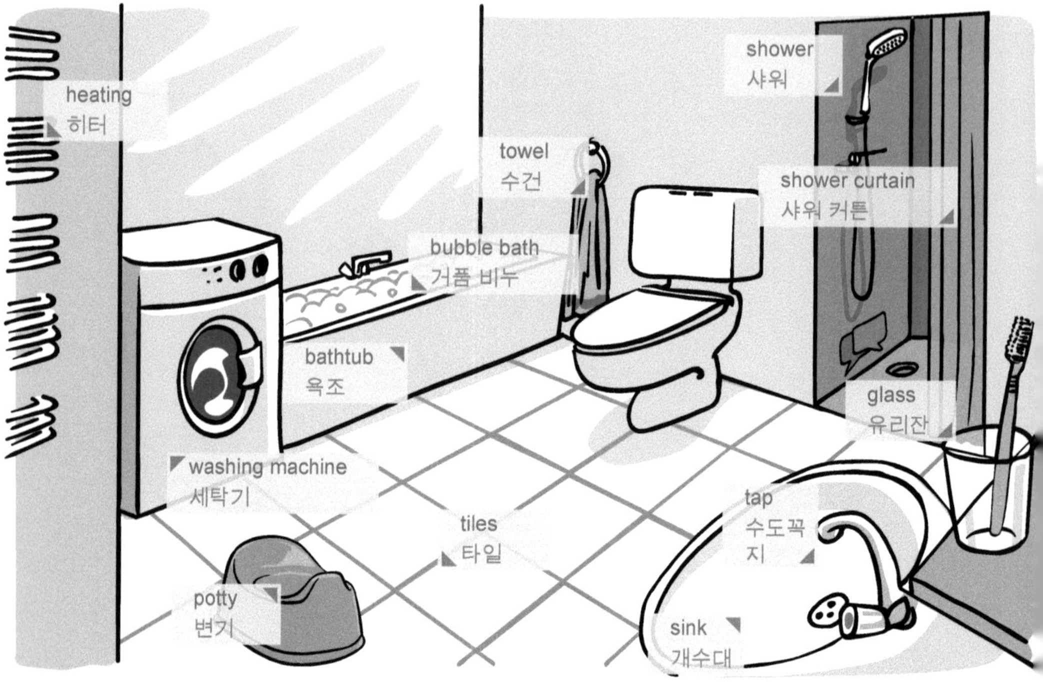
heating
히터
shower
샤워
towel
수건
shower curtain
샤워 커튼
bubble bath
거품 비누
bathtub
욕조
glass
유리잔
washing machine
세탁기
tap
수도꼭
지
tiles
타일
potty
변기
sink
개수대

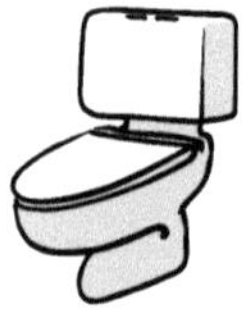

toilet
화장실

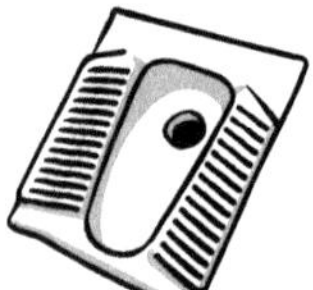

squat toilet
재래식 화장실

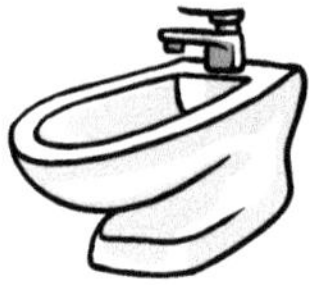

bidet
비데

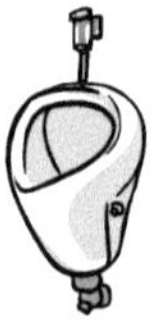

urinal
공중 변소

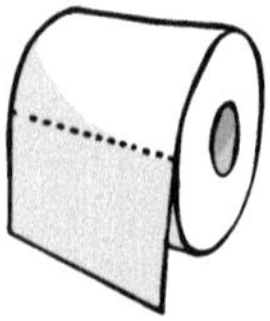

toilet paper
화장지

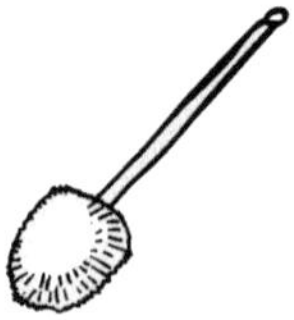

toilet brush
변기솔

toothbrush

치솔

toothpaste

치약

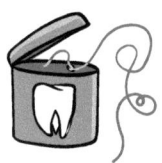

dental floss

치실

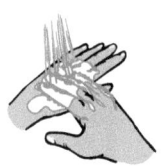

wash

씻다

handheld shower

샤워기

douche

질 세척제

basin

대야

back brush

등밀이솔

soap

비누

shower gel

샤워 젤

shampoo

샴푸

flannel

물걸레

drain

배수관

cream

크림

deodorant

체취 제거제

mirror

거울

hand mirror

휴대용 거울

razor

면도기

shaving foam

면도 거품

aftershave

에프터쉐이브

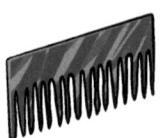

comb

빗

brush

솔

hair dryer

헤어드라이기

hairspray

헤어스프레이

makeup

메이크업

lipstick

립스틱

nail varnish

손톱깎이

cotton wool

면 솜

nail scissors

손톱

perfume

향수

washbag

세면도구 주머니

stool

스툴

weighing scale

저울

bathrobe

목욕 가운

rubber gloves

고무 장갑

tampon

탐폰

sanitary towel

생리대

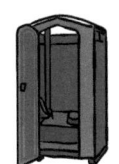

chemical toilet

화학 화장실

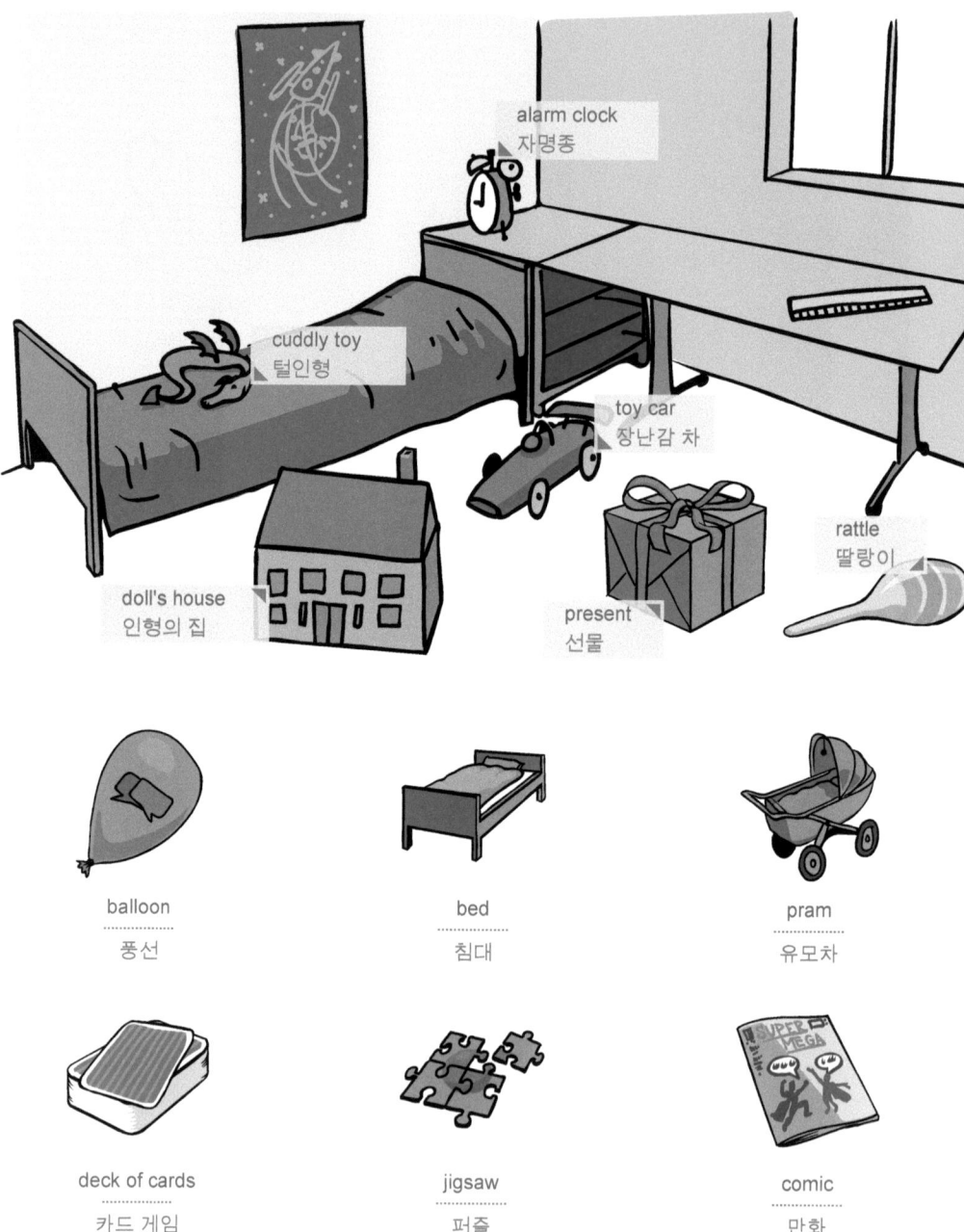

alarm clock
자명종

cuddly toy
털인형

toy car
장난감 차

rattle
딸랑이

doll's house
인형의 집

present
선물

balloon
풍선

bed
침대

pram
유모차

deck of cards
카드 게임

jigsaw
퍼즐

comic
만화

lego bricks

레고

building blocks

장난감 블럭

action figure

액션 캐릭터

babygrow

베이비 그로

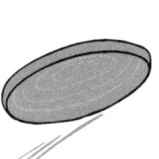

frisbee

프리스비

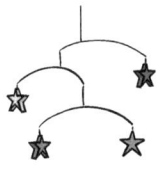

mobile

모빌

board game

보드 게임

dice

주사위

model train set

기차 모형 세트

dummy

노리개 젖꼭지

party

파티

picture book

그림책

ball

공

doll

인형

play

놀다

sandpit

모래상자

swing

그네

toys

장난감

video game console

비디오 게임 콘솔

tricycle

세바퀴자전거

teddy bear

곰인형

wardrobe

옷장

clothing

의복

socks

양말

stockings

스타킹

tights

스타킹

scarf
스카프

umbrella
우산

t-shirt
티셔츠

belt
허리띠

boots
부츠

slippers
슬리퍼

trainers
운동화

sandals	shoes	rubber boots
샌들	신발	고무 장화

underpants	bra	vest
팬티	브래지어	러닝 셔츠

body

바디

trousers

바지

jeans

청바지

skirt

치마

blouse

블라우스

shirt

셔츠

pullover

풀오버

hoodie

후드티

blazer

블레이저

jacket

자켓

coat

외투

raincoat

비옷

costume

의상

dress

원피스

wedding dress

웨딩 드레스

suit
양복

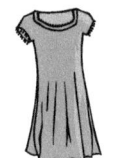

nightgown
나이트가운

pyjamas
잠옷

sari
사리

headscarf
두건

turban
터번

burqa
부르카

kaftan
카프탄

abaya
아바야

swimsuit
수영복

trunks
수영바지

shorts
반바지

tracksuit
트레이닝복

apron
앞치마

gloves
장갑

button
단추

glasses
안경

bracelet
팔찌

necklace
목걸이

ring
반지

earring
귀걸이

cap
캡 모자

coat hanger
옷걸이

hat
모자

tie
넥타이

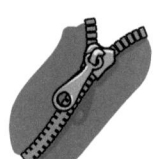

zip
지퍼

helmet
헬멧

braces
멜빵

school uniform
교복

uniform
유니폼

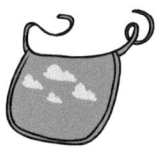

bib

턱받이

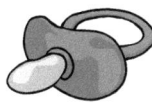

dummy

노리개 젖꼭지

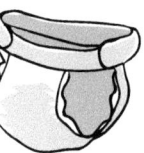

nappy

기저귀

office
사무실

server
서버
filing cabinet
서류 캐비닛
printer
인쇄기
paper
종이
monitor
모니터
mouse
마우스
desk
책상
folder
폴더
keyboard
자판기
waste-paper basket
휴지통
computer
컴퓨터
chair
의자

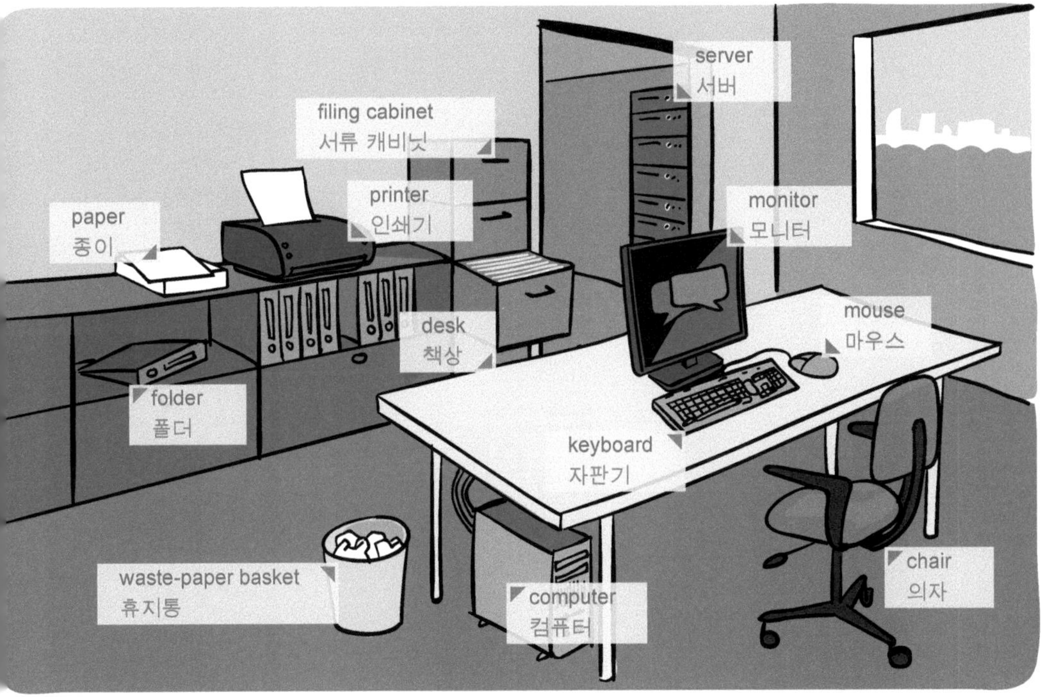

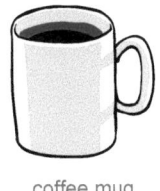

coffee mug

커피잔

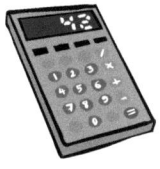

calculator

계산기

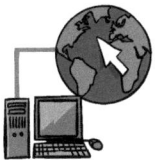

internet

인터넷

laptop

노트북

letter

편지

message

메시지

mobile

휴대전화

network

네트워크

photocopier

복사기

software

소프트웨어

telephone

전화

plug socket

플러그 소켓

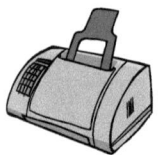

fax machine

팩시밀리

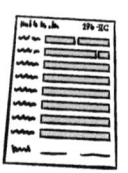

form

서식

document

서류

office - 사무실

buy

사다

pay

지불하다

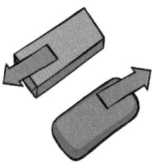

trade

거래하다

money

돈

dollar

달러

euro

유로

yen

엔

rouble

루벨

Swiss franc

스위스 프랑

renminbi yuan

위안

rupee

루피

cashpoint

현금인출기

bureau de change

환전소

gold

금

silver

은

oil

석유

energy

에너지

price

가격

contract

계약

tax

세금

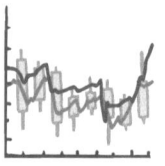

stock

주식

work

일하다

employee

근로자

employer

고용주

factory

공장

shop

상점

occupations
직업

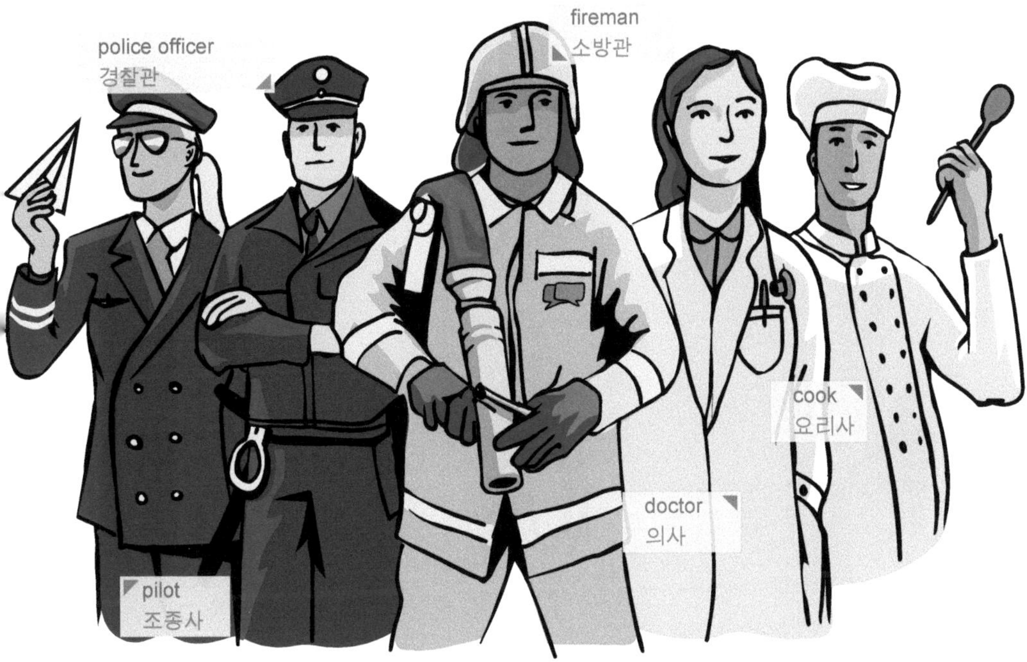

police officer
경찰관
fireman
소방관
pilot
조종사
doctor
의사
cook
요리사

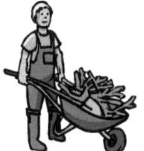

gardener

정원사

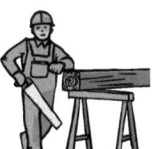

carpenter

목수

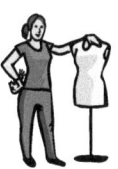

seamstress

수선공

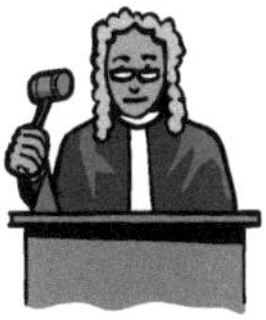

judge

판사

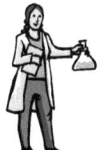

chemist

화학자

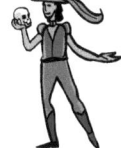

actor

배우

bus driver

버스운전사

taxi driver

택시 운전사

fisherman

어부

cleaning lady

청소부

roofer

지붕 수리자

waiter

웨이터

hunter

사냥꾼

painter

화가

baker

제빵사

electrician

전기업자

builder

건축업자

engineer

엔지니어

butcher

정육점업자

plumber

배관업자

postman

우편물 배달부

soldier

군인

architect

건축가

cashier

계산원

florist

플로리스트

hairdresser

미용사

conductor

검표원

mechanic

정비사

captain

선장

dentist

치과의사

scientist

학자

rabbi

유대교 라비

imam

이맘

monk

수도승

clergyman

사제

tools
연장

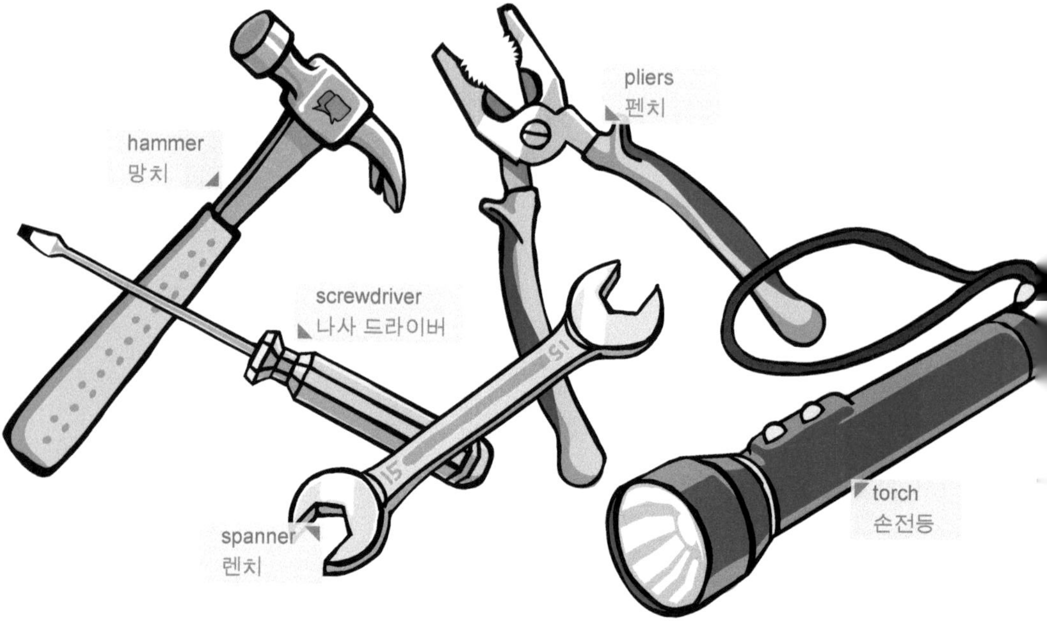
hammer
망치
pliers
펜치
screwdriver
나사 드라이버
spanner
렌치
torch
손전등

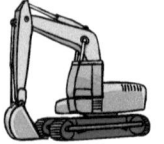

digger
굴삭기

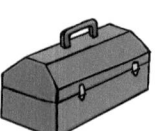

toolbox
연장통

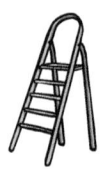

ladder
사다리

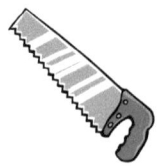

saw
톱

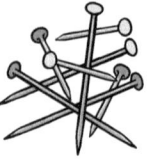

nails
못

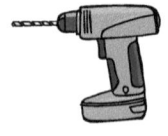

drill
드릴

repair

수리하다

shovel

삽

Damn!

젠장!

dustpan

쓰레받기

paint pot

페인트통

screws

나사

musical instruments
악기

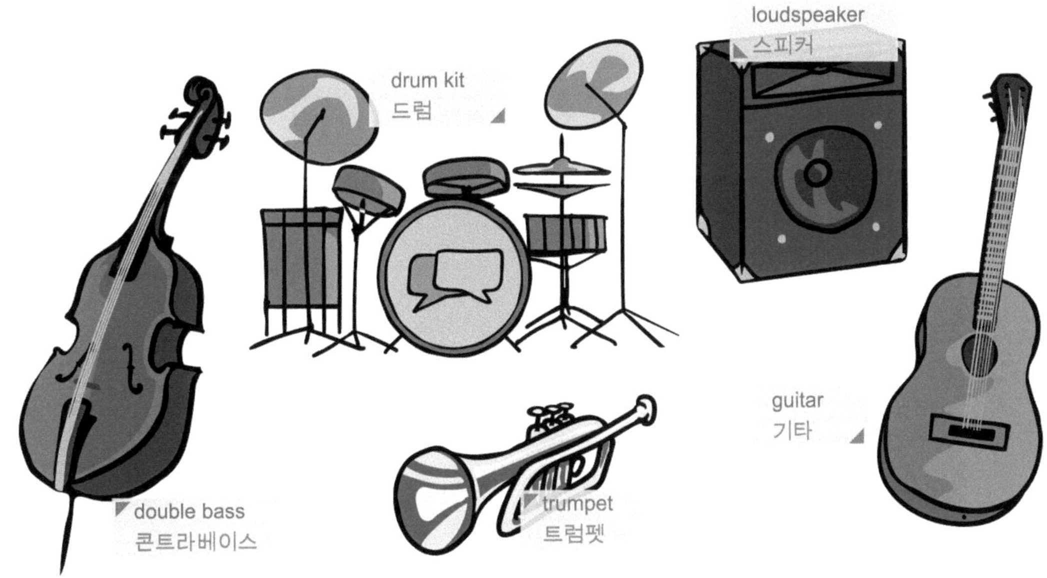

loudspeaker
스피커

drum kit
드럼

guitar
기타

double bass
콘트라베이스

trumpet
트럼펫

piano

피아노

violin

바이올린

bass

베이스

timpani

팀파니

drums

북

keyboard

키보드

saxophone

색소폰

flute

플루트

microphone

마이크

ZOO
동물원

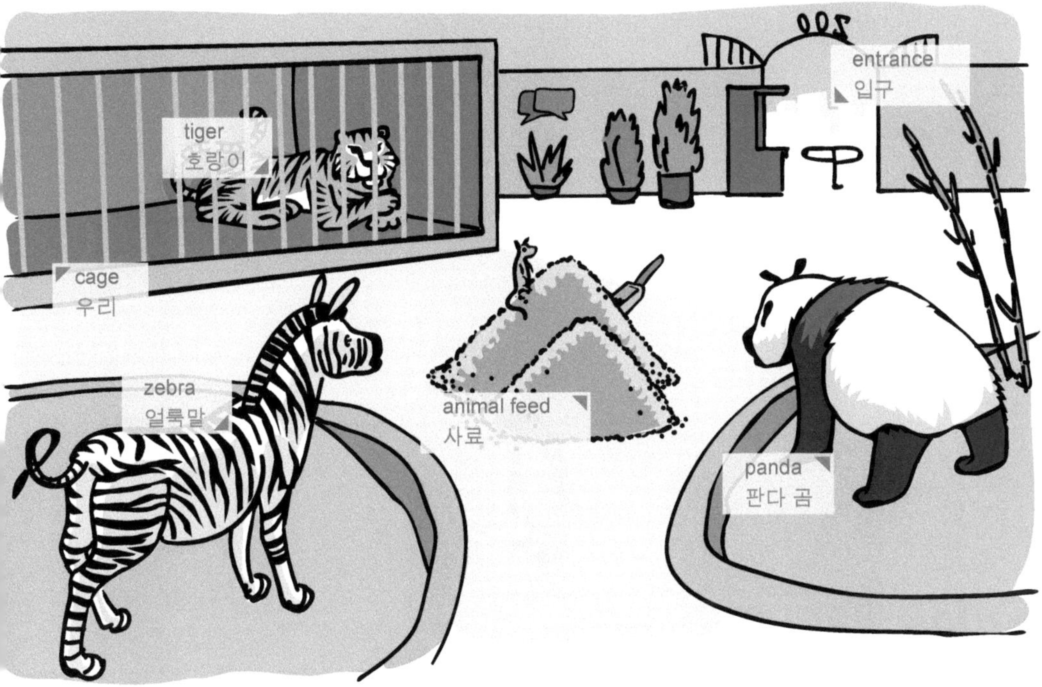
tiger
호랑이
entrance
입구
cage
우리
zebra
얼룩말
animal feed
사료
panda
판다 곰

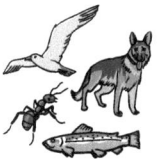

animals
동물

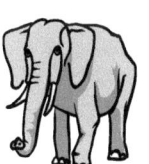

elephant
코끼리

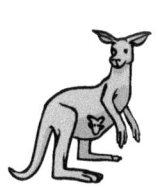

kangaroo
캥거루

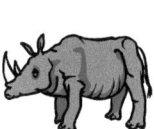

rhino
코뿔소

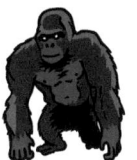

gorilla
고릴라

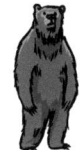

bear
곰

camel

낙타

ostrich

타조

lion

사자

monkey

원숭이

flamingo

홍학

parrot

앵무새

polar bear

북극곰

penguin

펭귄

shark

상어

peacock

공작

snake

뱀

crocodile

악어

zookeeper

동물원 사육사

seal

물개

jaguar

재규어

pony
조랑말

leopard
표범

hippo
하마

giraffe
기린

eagle
독수리

boar
맷돼지

fish
생선

turtle
거북이

walrus
바다코끼리

fox
여우

gazelle
영양

American football
미식축구

cycling
자전거
경기

tennis
테니스

basketball
농구

swimming
수영

boxing
권투

ice hockey
아이스하키

football
축구

badminton
배드민턴

athletics
육상 경기

handball
핸드볼

skiing
스키

polo
폴로

jump
뛰어오르
다

laugh
웃다

hug
포옹하
다

sing
노래하
다

walk
걷다

dream
꿈꾸다

pray
기도하
다

kiss
입맞추
다

write
쓰다

draw
그리다

show
보여주다

push
밀다

give
주다

take
받다

have

가지다

do

행하다

be

...이다

stand

서있다

run

뛰다

pull

당기다

throw

던지다

fall

떨어지다

lie

누워있다

wait

기다리다

carry

운반하다

sit

앉다

get dressed

옷을 입다

sleep

자다

wake up

깨다

activities - 활동

look at
보다

cry
울다

stroke
쓰다듬다

comb
빗다

talk
말하다

understand
이해하다

ask
묻다

listen
듣다

drink
마시다

eat
먹다

tidy up
정리하다

love
사랑하다

cook
요리하다

drive
주행하다

fly
날다

activities - 활동

sail

해항하다

calculate

계산하다

read

읽다

learn

배우다

work

일하다

marry

결혼하다

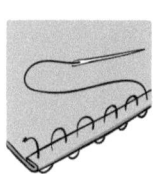

sew

바느질하다

brush teeth

이를 닦다

kill

죽이다

smoke

담배 피우다

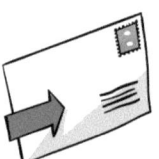

send

보내다

activities - 활동

family
가족

grandmother
할머니

grandfather
할아버지

father
아버지

mother
어머니

baby
아기

daughter
딸

son
아들

guest
손님

aunt
이모 / 고모

uncle
삼촌

brother
형제

sister
자매

family - 가족

67

body
몸통

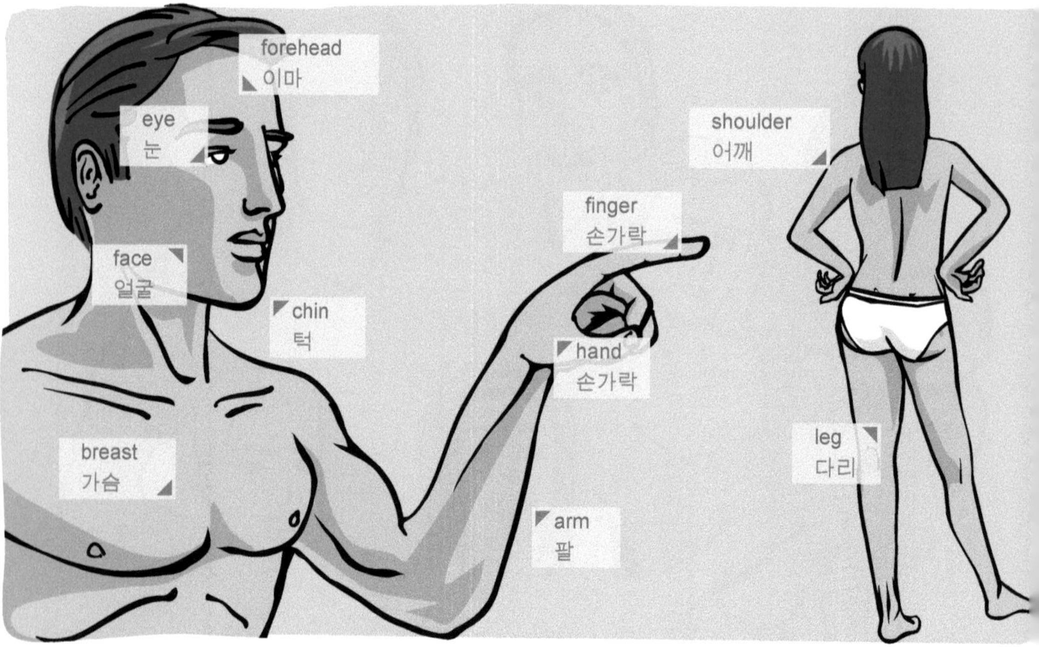

forehead
이마

eye
눈

shoulder
어깨

finger
손가락

face
얼굴

chin
턱

hand
손가락

breast
가슴

leg
다리

arm
팔

baby

아기

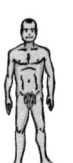

man

남자

woman

여자

girl

소녀

boy

소년

head

머리카락

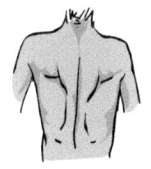

back

둥

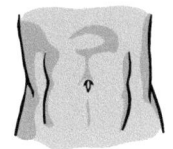

belly

배

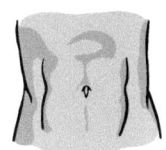

belly button

배꼽

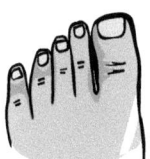

toe

발가락

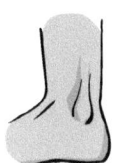

heel

발꿈치

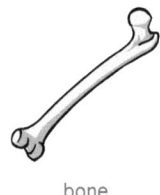

bone

뼈

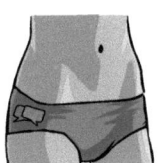

hip

엉덩이

knee

무릎

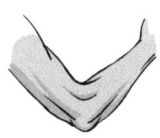

elbow

팔꿈치

nose

코

bottom

둔부

skin

피부

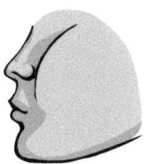

cheek

뺨

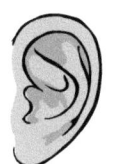

ear

귀

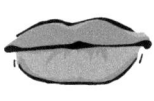

lip

입술

mouth

입

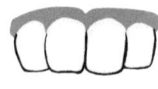

tooth

치아

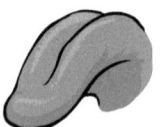

tongue

혀

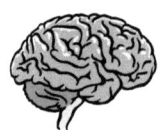

brain

뇌

heart

심장

muscle

근육

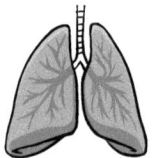

lung

허파

liver

간

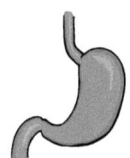

stomach

위

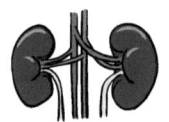

kidneys

신장

sex

성교

condom

콘돔

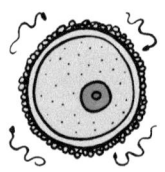

ovum

난자

semen

정자

pregnancy

임신

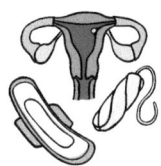

menstruation
월경

vagina
질

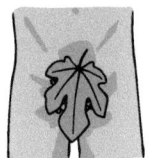

penis
음경

eyebrow
눈썹

hair
머리카락

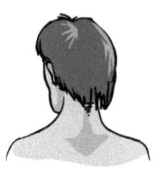

neck
목

hospital
병원

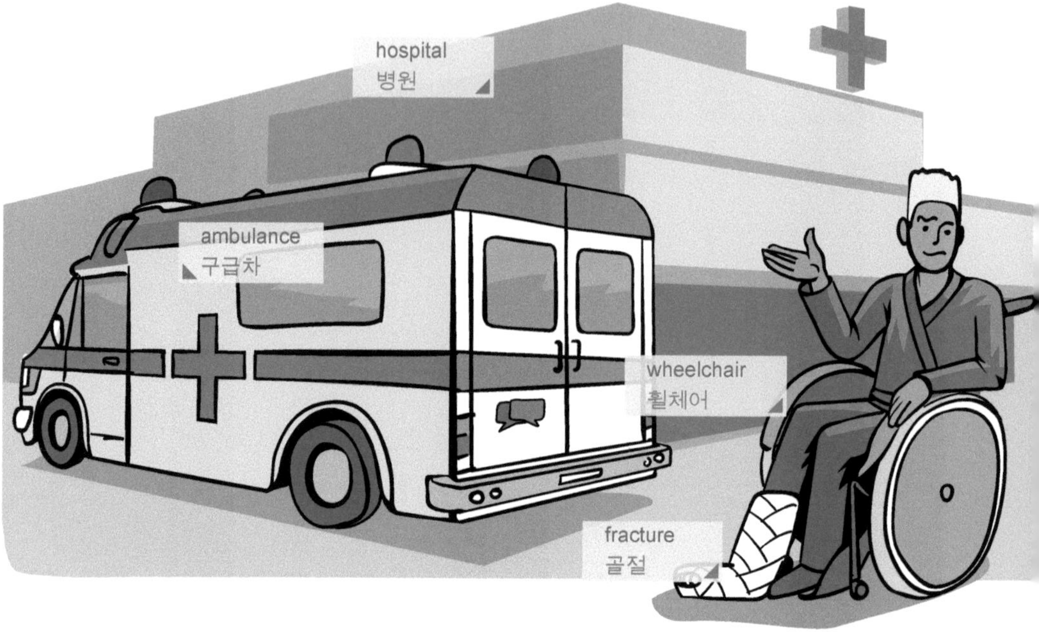

hospital
병원
ambulance
구급차
wheelchair
휠체어
fracture
골절

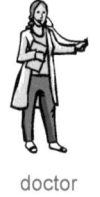

doctor
의사

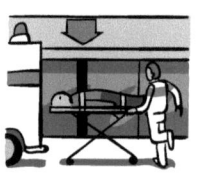

emergency room
응급실

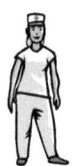

nurse
간호사

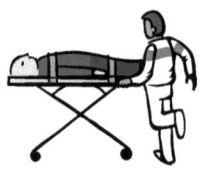

emergency
응급상황

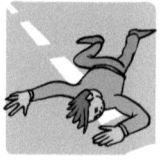

unconscious
혼수상태

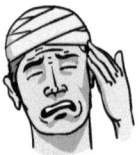

pain
통증

injury
부상

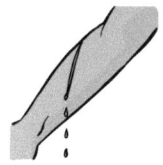

bleeding
출혈

heart attack
심장마비

stroke
뇌졸중

allergy
알러지

cough
기침

fever
열

flu
독감

diarrhoea
설사

headache
두통

cancer
암

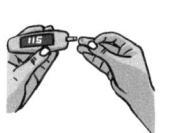

diabetes
당뇨병

surgeon
외과의

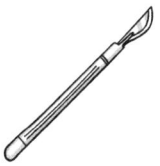

scalpel
수술용 메스

operation
수술

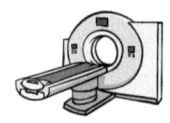

CT

CT

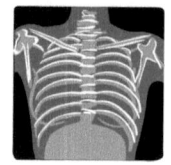

x-ray

엑스레이

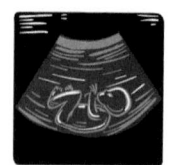

ultrasound

초음파

face mask

마스크

disease

질병

waiting room

대기실

crutch

목발

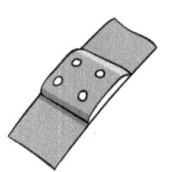

plaster

반창고

bandage

붕대

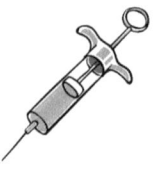

injection

주사

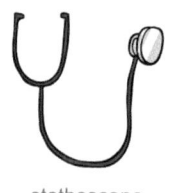

stethoscope

청진기

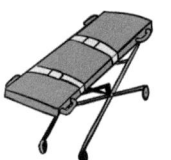

stretcher

들것

clinical thermometer

체온계

birth

출생

overweight

과체중

74   hospital - 병원

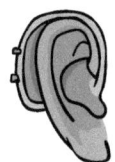

hearing aid
....
보청기

disinfectant
....
소독약

infection
....
감염

virus
....
바이러스

HIV / AIDS
....
HIV / AIDS

medicine
....
의학

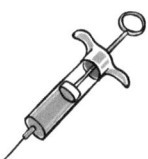

vaccination
....
예방접종

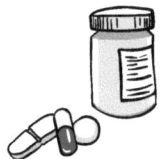

tablets
....
알약

pill
....
알약

emergency call
....
구급 전화

blood pressure monitor
....
혈압측정기

ill / healthy
....
병든 / 건강한

Help!

도와주세요!

alarm

경보음

assault

폭행

attack

공격

danger

위험

emergency exit

비상구

Fire!

불이야!

fire extinguisher

소화기

accident

사고

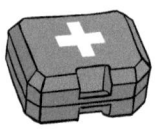

first-aid kit

구급 상자

SOS

SOS

police

경찰

Europe

유럽

North America

북미

South America

남미

Africa

아프리카

Asia

아시아

Australia

호주

Atlantic

북극

Pacific

태평양

Indian Ocean

인도양

Antarctic Ocean

남극해

Arctic Ocean

북극해

North Pole

북극해

South Pole
남극해

Antarctica
남극

Earth
지구

land
육지

sea
바다

island
섬

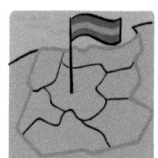

nation
국가

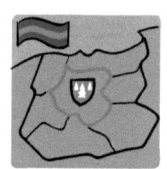

state
주

clock face

시계 문자판

hour hand

시침

minute hand

분침

second hand

초침

What time is it?

몇 시입니까?

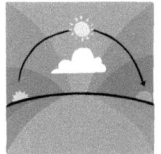

day

일

time

시간

now

지금

digital watch

디지털 시계

minute

분

hour

시간

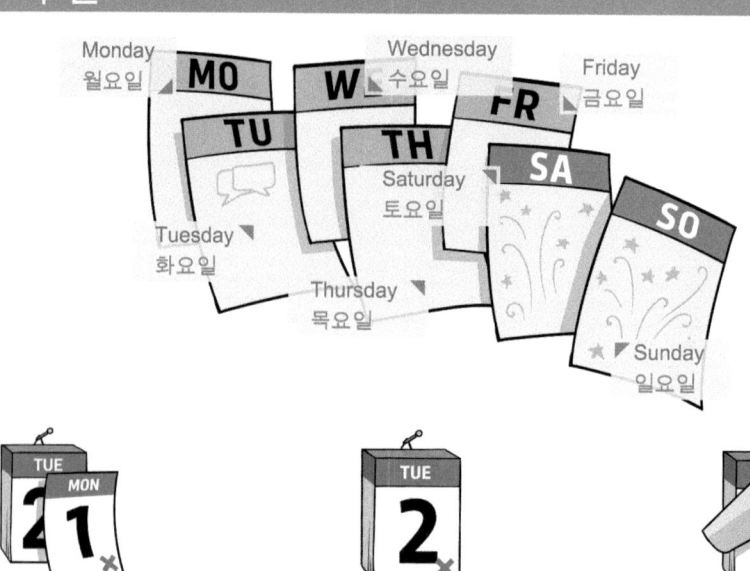

Monday
월요일

Tuesday
화요일

Wednesday
수요일

Thursday
목요일

Friday
금요일

Saturday
토요일

Sunday
일요일

yesterday

어제

today

오늘

tomorrow

내일

morning

아침

noon

정오

evening

저녁

business days

근로일

weekend

주말

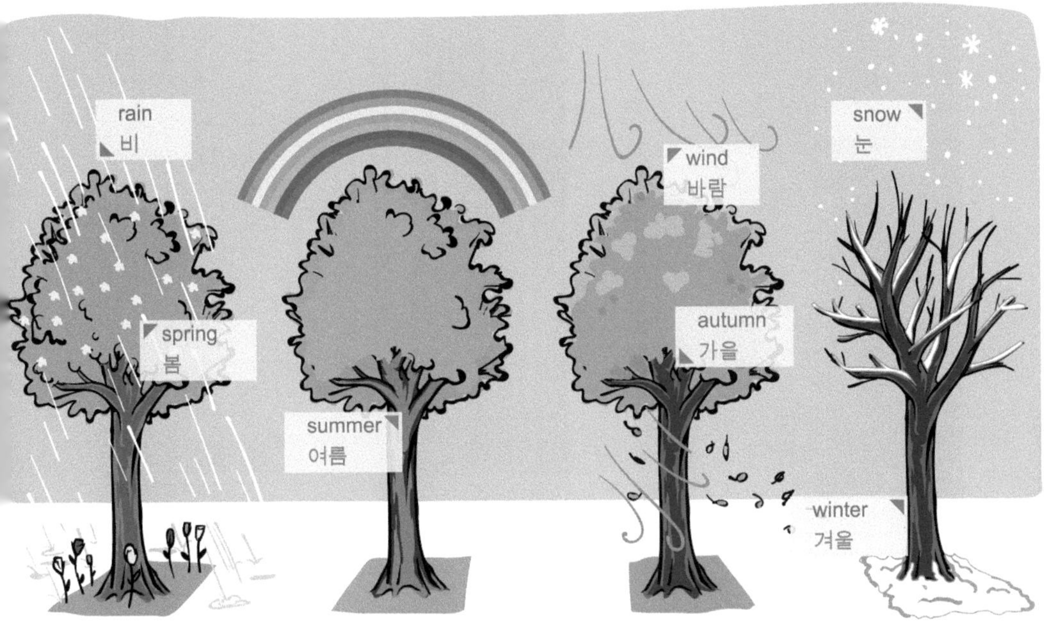

rain
비
wind
바람
snow
눈
spring
봄
autumn
가을
summer
여름
winter
겨울

4.APRIL 11°
5.APRIL 4°
6.APRIL 13°
7.APRIL 8°
8.APRIL 10°

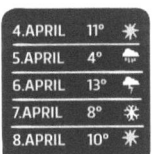

weather forecast
날씨 예보

F C
120 40
90 30
60 20
30 10
0 0
-30 -10
-20

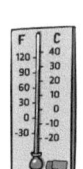

thermometer
온도계

sunshine
햇빛

cloud
구름

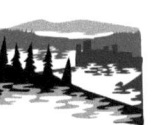

fog
안개

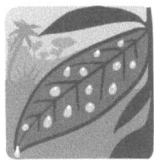

humidity
습도

lightning

번개

thunder

천둥

storm

폭풍

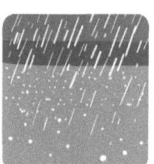

hail

우박

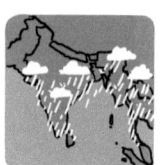

monsoon

장마

flood

홍수

ice

얼음

January

1월

February

2월

March

3월

April

4월

May

5월

June

6월

July

7월

August

8월

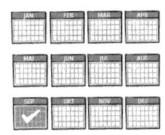

September

9월

October

10월

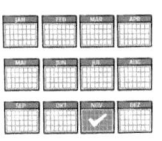

November

11월

December

12월

circle

원

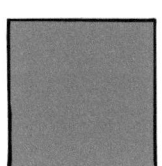

square

정사각형

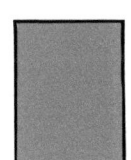

rectangle

직사각형

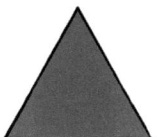

triangle

삼각형

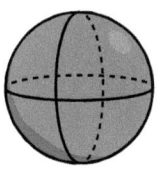

sphere

구

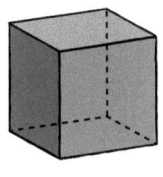

cube

정사면체

colours
색

white
하양

yellow
노랑

orange
주황

pink
분홍

red
빨강

purple
보라

blue
파랑

green
초록

brown
갈색

grey
회색

black
검정

a lot / a little

많은 / 적은

angry / calm

화난 / 차분한

beautiful / ugly

아름다운 / 추한

beginning / end

시작 / 끝

big / small

큰 / 작은

bright / dark

밝은 / 어두운

brother / sister

형제 / 자매

clean / dirty

깨끗한 / 더러운

complete / incomplete

완전한 / 불완전한

day / night

낮 / 밤

dead / alive

죽은 / 산

wide / narrow

넓은 / 좁은

edible / inedible

삭용의 / 비식용의

evil / kind

불친절한 / 친절한

excited / bored

흥분된 / 지루한

fat / thin

뚱뚱한 / 마른

first / last

처음으로 / 마지막으로

friend / enemy

친구 / 적

full / empty

꽉 찬 / 텅 빈

hard / soft

딱딱한 / 부드러운

heavy / light

무거운 / 가벼운

hunger / thirst

배고픔 / 목마름

ill / healthy

병든 / 건강한

illegal / legal

불법 / 합법

intelligent / stupid

영리한 / 어리석은

left / right

왼 / 오른

near / far

가까운 / 먼

opposites - 반대

new / used
새 / 헌

nothing / something
무 / 유

old / young
늙은 / 젊은

on / off
온 / 오프

open / closed
열린 / 닫힌

quiet / loud
조용한 / 시끄러운

rich / poor
부유한 / 가난한

right / wrong
옳은 / 틀린

rough / smooth
거친 / 매끄러운

sad / happy
슬픈 / 기쁜

short / long
짧은 / 긴

slow / fast
느린 / 빠른

wet / dry
젖은 / 마른

warm / cool
따뜻한 / 시원한

war / peace
전쟁 / 평화

opposites - 반대

0	**1**	**2**
zero	one	two
영	하나	둘

3	**4**	**5**
three	four	five
셋	넷	다섯

6	**7**	**8**
six	seven	eight
여섯	일곱	여덟

9	**10**	**11**
nine	ten	eleven
아홉	열	열하나

12

twelve
열둘

13

thirteen
열셋

14

fourteen
열넷

15

fifteen
열다섯

16

sixteen
열여섯

17

seventeen
열일곱

18

eighteen
열여덟

19

nineteen
열아홉

20

twenty
스물

100

hundred
백

1.000

thousand
천

1.000.000

million
백만

languages
언어

English
영어

American English
미국식 영어

Chinese Mandarin
중국어 만다린

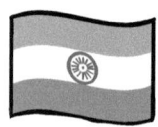

Hindi
힌두어

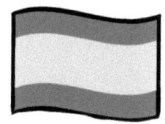

Spanish
스페인어

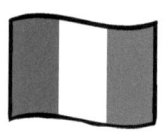

French
프랑스어

Arabic
아랍어

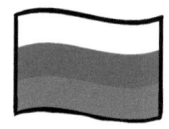

Russian
러시아어

Portuguese
포르투갈어

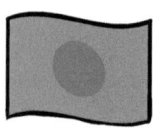

Bengali
불가리아어

German
독일어

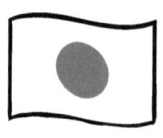

Japanese
일본어

I

나

you

너

he / she / it

그 / 그녀/ 그것

we

우리

you

너희들

they

그들

who?

누가?

what?

무엇이?

how?

어떻게?

where?

어디서?

when?

언제?

name

이름

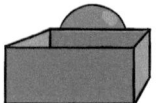

behind
뒤에

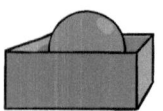

in
안에

in front of
앞에

over
위에

on
위에

under
아래에

beside
옆에

between
사이에

place
장소